Dearest Andrew,

HAPPY BIRTHDAY !!
&
HAPPY COOKING !!

Love,
Sam xxx

The little book with a big heart

Food photography by Chris Terry
Design by superfantastic

✱ 25% of the net proceeds from The Big Feastival will be paid to Prince's Trust Trading Limited. PTT Ltd covenants all its taxable profits to The Prince's Trust, a registered charity incorporated by Royal Charter in England and Wales (1079675) and Scotland (SC041198). 75% of profits from The Big Feastival will be paid to the Jamie Oliver Foundation (registered charity number 1094536).

Contents

Recipes

Hi guys,

Welcome to The Big Feastival and thank you for buying this cookbook. All of the profits will go directly to helping young people through my charity, the Jamie Oliver Foundation, and The Prince's Trust, founded by His Royal Highness The Prince of Wales, which has been a constant inspiration to me.

The Prince's Trust is one of Britain's very best charities and social enterprises. HRH The Prince of Wales is incredibly passionate about giving opportunities to young people from all walks of life, to help them realise their full potential. Over the years, I've met loads of brilliant young people who've had that little moment where grants of cash, help with key equipment or a bit of guidance has helped them on their journeys to realising how amazing they can be. I've seen first-hand how these youngsters really reap the benefits.

2012 marks the 10th anniversary of the Fifteen Apprentice Programme. We've had more than 400 students work in our restaurants, many of whom have come from challenging backgrounds. Loads of them have gone on to carve out amazing careers as professional chefs, both in the UK and abroad. And they're always kept in the fold of the Fifteen family, so we can keep up that mentoring process and help them with their future needs.

Ultimately, both charities are about sharing the love of people, and realising that, whoever you are, what's truly important is creating a culture where everyone treats others as they'd like to be treated. And that's where all the proceeds of this book and this whole Big Feastival event will go, because giving people a break and opportunities at that crucial time in their lives costs cash. So I can't emphasise enough how important your contribution is.

You're here and you're experiencing it all – Feastival is bringing together great food, great chefs, great music and all sorts of wonderful artisans and craftsmen. I'm full of gratitude and respect for all of my brothers and sisters who have contributed to this fine, cute cookbook. We've got fantastic recipes from some of the best in the business including Sophie Grigson, who's inspired me for so many years, and the one and only Giorgio Locatelli, one of London's best Italian chefs. There's Theo Randall, who was my boss, and head chef at the River Café for many years, the brilliant Jonathan Downey at Redhook, who's sorting the bar for us, Atul Kochhar, who's really raised the stakes with Indian food, and Peter Gordon at The Providores (or for old-school guys like me, from The Sugar Club), who's at the heart of London's food and restaurant scene. We've got the Women's Institute representing and the Shoreditch Sisters, one of the strong clans of the WI, who are helping to head up the WI tent. We've got an army of gorgeous no-nonsense girls like the lovely Rachel Allen, my dear friend

Jo Pratt and, of course, the wonderful Thomasina Miers, who has had huge success with her Wahaca Mexican restaurants. There's Andrew Parkinson, our executive head chef at Fifteen, who does an incredible job of looking after our students, and Adam Perry Lang, one of the world's best barbecue guys and my partner at Barbecoa. We've also got some fantastic restaurants and cooks being represented from John Murray at Vinoteca, Adam Byatt at Trinity and the guys at Café Spice Namasté to Canteen and Gourmet Burger Kitchen.

Thank you to all of our wonderful contributors for being ambassadors for the best in British cooking. I hope you, the recipient of this lovely book, will enjoy all the different styles and flavours represented here.

And, most of all, enjoy the first ever Feastival. It's all for charity so get stuck in and enjoy yourself.

Big love,

James

The Jamie Oliver Foundation

The mission of the Jamie Oliver Foundation is to empower, educate and engage as many people as possible to love and enjoy good food. This means learning how to cook, understanding where food comes from, and recognising the power it can have on our health, happiness, and even finances. We do this through teaching, training and employment, and by making good, clear information available to as many people as possible.

The Foundation is a registered charity, governed by a board of trustees who all passionately believe that food can make an empowering and lasting difference to the lives of every person. Jamie is the driving force behind the Foundation. Under the UK Foundation, there are three charity activities:

Fifteen's Apprentice Programme
Jamie's School Projects
Jamie's Ministry of Food

Fifteen's Apprentice Programme

In 2002, Jamie founded Fifteen, a restaurant group that uses the magic of food to give unemployed young people a chance for a better future. The group is made up of three restaurants: the flagship Fifteen London, Fifteen Amsterdam and Fifteen Cornwall.

At the heart of the business is a desire to encourage young people to believe in themselves, to show each one of them their past can be left behind and persuade them that they can create their own future. To date, more than 220 apprentices have graduated, many of whom have carved out successful careers in the restaurant industry all over the world.

Jamie's School Projects

In 2005, Jamie's Channel 4 television series *Jamie's School Dinners* highlighted the poor quality of meals provided by the majority of UK schools. Jamie's Feed Me Better campaign, which ran alongside the series, led to major investment by the government as well as policy changes to improve school food. Jamie continues his campaigning role in relation to the school food agenda.

Jamie's Ministry of Food

In 2008, Jamie launched his Ministry of Food campaign with the aim of getting people cooking again. He wanted to encourage people to share their cooking skills, teach their friends what they had learnt, and prove that anyone could learn to cook. He also wanted to show that it was fun, cool, could save them money and help their families and friends to live healthier lives.

To date, there are three Ministry of Food centres in the UK, and one mobile outreach programme. A further two centres are due to open in late 2011.

www.jamieoliver.com/foundation

Jamie Oliver Foundation

The Prince's Trust

The Prince's Trust is a charity for 14- to 30-year-olds who have struggled at school, have been in care, are long-term unemployed or have been in trouble with the law. Around one in five young people in the UK are not in work, education or training. Youth unemployment costs the UK economy £10 million a day in lost productivity, while youth crime costs £1 billion every year.

The Prince's Trust addresses this by giving practical and financial support to the young people who need it the most. The charity helps develop key skills, confidence and motivation, enabling young people to move into work, education or training. HRH The Prince of Wales's charity has helped more than 600,000 young people since 1976 and supports 100 more each working day. Last year, 81 per cent of young people supported by The Trust moved into work, education, training or volunteering.

The Prince's Trust Get Into programme is a series of short vocational courses in sectors such as cooking and hospitality. Last year, 1,837 disadvantaged young people took part in a Get Into programme and 74 per cent of those who completed the course achieved positive outcomes including employment, further education or training and voluntary work.

The Prince's Trust's other key activity is Get Started, a programme of arts and music designed to engage young people who are significantly alienated from education, training and employment and lack the confidence, motivation or skills to move forward. Get Started With Music gives young people unique opportunities such as working with professional musicians and developing their skills in vocals, instruments or music technology. Last year, 76 per cent of the 1,238 people who took part in a Get Started programme achieved positive outcomes.

www.princes-trust.org.uk

Prince's Trust

SOPHIE GRIGSON

"Muhammara" is the Middle Eastern name for this beautiful brick-red pepper and walnut purée, a kissing cousin of hummus. It's laced with ground cumin and pomegranate molasses, which give it a fabulous tart, fruity flavour.

Red pepper & walnut purée

- 4 red peppers
- 2 fresh red chillies
- 100g walnuts, toasted
- 40g good-quality white bread, ripped into small pieces
- 2 teaspoons ground cumin
- 2 garlic cloves, peeled and roughly chopped
- 1 tablespoon pomegranate molasses, available from good delis and some supermarkets
- 150ml extra virgin olive oil
- sea salt

Grill the peppers and the chillies either in a griddle pan, under the grill, on the barbecue or over the flame of your gas hob, turning with tongs, until blackened and blistered all over. Drop into a plastic bag, seal and leave until cool enough to handle. Pull out and throw away the stems, then pull away the skins of both peppers and chillies. Quarter and deseed the peppers; halve and deseed the chillies.

Put the peppers and chillies into the bowl of a food processor together with all the remaining ingredients (except the oil). Pulse process until everything is fairly finely chopped. Set the motor running constantly, and pour in the oil. Taste and adjust the seasoning – it needs more salt than you'd imagine. Scrape into a bowl. Serve with batons of carrots, radishes and celery, and warm flatbread, or in sandwiches.

Recipe taken from *Spices* by Sophie Grigson, published autumn 2011 (Quadrille Publishing).

LOCANDA LOCATELLI
GIORGIO LOCATELLI

Known in Italy as "caponata di melanzane", this Sicilian dish just explodes in your mouth. Its vinegary flavour makes it the perfect accompaniment to roast meat, such as lamb, because it cuts through the fattiness, but it is also traditionally served with seafood.

Sweet & sour aubergine

SERVES 4

- 1 large aubergine (roughly 400g)
- sea salt and freshly ground black pepper
- 1 red onion, peeled
- 1 tablespoon olive oil
- 2 celery sticks, trimmed
- ½ fennel bulb, trimmed
- vegetable oil (roughly 2 litres), for deep-frying
- 75 to 125ml extra virgin olive oil
- 75ml good-quality red wine vinegar
- 3 ripe plum tomatoes
- 50g sultanas
- 50g pine nuts
- 2 teaspoons caster sugar
- small bunch of fresh basil, leaves picked

Cut the aubergine into 2cm dice, place in a colander, sprinkle generously with salt and leave to drain for at least 2 hours. Meanwhile, cut the onion into 1cm dice. Heat the olive oil in a frying pan, add the onion and sauté until soft, then transfer to a large bowl and set aside. Cut the celery, then the fennel into 1cm dice and place them in separate bowls.

Rinse the aubergine well and drain thoroughly. Heat the vegetable oil in a large, deep saucepan until it is hot enough to brown a cube of bread in 1 minute (remember hot oil can be dangerous, so be careful and keep an eye on it). Add the diced celery and fry for 1 to 2 minutes or until tender and golden. Remove with a slotted spoon and drain on a plate lined with kitchen paper. Repeat with the diced fennel, then the diced aubergine.

Add the deep-fried vegetables to the onion bowl. Add the extra virgin olive oil and red wine vinegar, then season to taste. Cut the tomatoes into 2cm dice and add to the bowl along with the sultanas, pine nuts and sugar. Chop and add the basil leaves, then stir to combine the ingredients. Cover the bowl and leave to infuse at room temperature for at least 2 hours before eating. Serve piled high on chunks of fresh, crusty bread or with plenty of mozzarella or fried artichokes.

Recipe © Locanda Locatelli – Giorgio Locatelli

TRINITY
ADAM BYATT

The simple things in life are often the best when it comes to selecting the ideal food to enjoy outdoors: my favourites are chilled soups, fresh tomatoes, crusty bread and, of course, plenty of smelly cheeses. A picnic isn't a success without sticky fingers and a huge mess to shake off the rug afterwards!

English pea & mint soup

SERVES
8

- 1kg fresh English peas, in the pod
- few sprigs of fresh thyme
- 1 fresh bay leaf
- 1 small onion, peeled and finely sliced
- 25g unsalted butter
- sea salt and freshly ground black pepper
- 500ml single cream
- 500ml milk
- 1 sprig of fresh mint

To serve (optional)
- 8 teaspoons good-quality olive oil, 8 heaped teaspoons crème fraîche and 60g pea shoots

Pod the peas; set the peas aside, then wash the pods. Add the pods, thyme sprigs and bay leaf to a large saucepan with 1 litre of cold water. Bring to the boil over a high heat, then reduce to a simmer for 25 minutes. Strain the stock through a colander set over a bowl, then discard the pods and herbs and reserve the liquid.

Sweat the onion with the butter in a large saucepan over a low heat and season well. Once the onions are soft, add the reserved stock, cream and milk and bring to the boil (you must do this before adding the peas to preserve the vibrant pea colour). Add the reserved peas to the boiling liquid and cook for 4 minutes, or until tender, then remove from the heat. While the soup is still hot, blend carefully with a stick blender for 4 minutes, or until smooth.

Pass the soup through a fine sieve into a large bowl with the mint in it to infuse the soup. Refrigerate, over ice if possible, until ready to serve chilled.

Before serving, remove the mint and skim off any scum from the surface. Serve garnished with olive oil, crème fraîche, black pepper and pea shoots, if you like.

PS. This soup also tastes great when served warm.

JAMIE OLIVER

This is one of my all-time favourite salads. I love the combination of soft and crunchy textures, and the contrast between the sweet roasted squash and the salty feta. Keep the elements separate, then assemble just before serving to ensure everything stays lovely and fresh.

Roasted squash & feta salad

SERVES
4

- 1 large butternut squash
- olive oil
- sea salt and freshly ground black pepper
- ½ teaspoon dried oregano
- 1 dried red chilli
- 2 ripe avocados
- juice of 1 lemon
- extra virgin olive oil
- 4 spring onions, trimmed
- 2 tablespoons pumpkin seeds
- ½ teaspoon cumin seeds
- large handful of pea shoots, washed and spun dry
- ½ bunch of fresh mint, leaves picked
- 100g feta

Preheat your oven to 200°C/400°F/gas 6. Halve the squash, then deseed and get rid of any gnarly bits of skin (there's no need to peel it). Cut the squash into 3cm chunks and place in a large roasting tray. Drizzle with a lug of olive oil and season well. Sprinkle with the oregano, crumble over the chilli and toss everything together until mixed well. Roast for 40 to 45 minutes, or until the squash is golden and cooked through.

Meanwhile, halve the avocados, remove the stones and discard, then finely slice the flesh. Place in a large bowl with the lemon juice and the same amount of extra virgin olive oil. Finely slice the spring onions and add to the bowl, then season well.

Leave the roasted squash to cool for 5 minutes. Meanwhile, toast the pumpkin and cumin seeds in a hot, dry pan for a couple of minutes, or until golden and smelling fantastic. Add the seeds to the avocado bowl with the squash, pea shoots and mint leaves, then toss together. Spread the salad out on a serving platter and crumble over the feta.

PS: If you're a bit of a meat fiend, you could add some crispy pancetta to the mix.

REDHOOK
JONATHAN
DOWNEY

I could eat these prawns just about every day in the summer. They're so simple to make and go great with a nicely chilled glass (or two) of crisp white wine and plenty of lovely sunshine.

Pink peppercorn prawns

SERVES
4

- 12 large raw tiger prawns, shell on
- juice of 1 lemon
- juice of 1 orange
- sea salt
- white wine vinegar
- ½ teaspoon fennel seeds
- 2 star anise
- extra virgin olive oil
- basil cress, to serve

For the dressing
- few sprigs of fresh basil, leaves picked
- 5g pink peppercorns
- 1 large garlic clove, peeled
- zest of ½ lemon and 1 teaspoon of juice
- 1 teaspoon lime juice
- 65ml grapeseed oil

Preheat your grill to low. Peel all the prawns, leaving the tails intact. Put a pan of water on to simmer and season it with the lemon and orange juices, a pinch of salt, a splash of white wine vinegar, the fennel seeds and star anise. Blanch the prawns in the simmering water for 20 seconds, then refresh in a bowl of ice-cold water.

Slice each prawn down its back and devein. Lay the prawns on a roasting tray, tail-side up, and drizzle with a little extra virgin olive oil. Gently warm under the grill until pink and cooked through.

Meanwhile, for the dressing, bring the same pan of water to the boil, blanch most of the basil leaves for 2 seconds, then refresh in iced water. Blitz the basil, using a stick blender, with the rest of the dressing ingredients until smooth. Very finely slice the remaining basil leaves.

Place the prawns on a plate with their tails up. Serve them warm with a drizzle of the dressing and a sprinkle of salt, sliced basil leaves and basil cress.

CAFÉ SPICE NAMASTÉ
PERVIN & CYRUS TODIWALA

This is a fantastically simple but flavoursome fish curry that doesn't require much preparation. Pomfret is used in India to give the best flavour to this dish, but any sustainable white fish will do. Serve with plenty of poppadoms and plain rice for "mopping up" the sauce.

Parsee green fish curry

SERVES
4

- 2 tablespoons sunflower oil
- 1 onion, peeled and finely sliced
- 4 garlic cloves, peeled and finely grated
- 4cm piece of fresh ginger, peeled and finely grated
- 2 fresh green chillies, deseeded and finely chopped
- ½ teaspoon ground turmeric
- 400ml tin of coconut milk
- sea salt
- 4 green cardamom pods, lightly crushed
- 4 cloves
- 5 to 6 curry leaves
- 2cm piece of cinnamon stick
- 4 fish steaks or 400g thick skinless white fish fillet, cut into large chunks
- ½ bunch of fresh coriander, leaves picked and chopped

Heat the oil in a large pan over a low heat. Add the onion and cook for a few minutes until translucent, but not coloured. Add the garlic, ginger and chilli and cook for a further minute or two (do not let them brown). Stir in the turmeric, cook for a few seconds, then stir in the coconut milk. Bring to a steady simmer over a medium heat, stirring frequently right from the bottom of the pan.

Add a pinch of salt, then the cardamom, cloves, curry leaves and cinnamon stick. Simmer, uncovered, for a few minutes or until the sauce has thickened slightly.

Add the fish and most of the coriander and cook for 2 to 4 minutes (depending on the thickness of the steaks or chunks of fish). Cover the pan, remove from the heat and let the fish finish cooking in the residual heat of the curry for 4 to 5 minutes. Sprinkle with the remaining coriander before serving.

Recipe © Cyrus Todiwala

REDHOOK
JONATHAN DOWNEY

This is a wonderfully delicious combination of seafood and meat that has always been a favourite with my kids, whatever the time of year. Of course, they're a hit with adults too!

Seared scallops & chorizo

SERVES 2

- 6 diver scallops, preferably in the shell
- I red pepper
- 60g good-quality cooking chorizo
- 6 sprigs of fresh flat-leaf parsley, leaves picked and very finely sliced
- olive oil
- red wine
- balsamic vinegar
- sea salt and freshly ground black pepper
- juice of I lemon

Carefully remove the scallops from their shells (if still attached) with a small palette knife. Discard the roe and soak the scallops in iced water until firm, then set aside.

Grill the pepper either in a griddle pan, under the grill, on the barbecue or over the flame of your gas hob, turning with tongs, until blackened and blistered all over. Drop it into a plastic bag, seal and set aside for about 20 minutes. When cool enough to handle, take out the pepper, pull away its skin and stem and discard. Deseed and cut into ½cm dice, then set aside.

Cut the chorizo into ½cm dice, then set aside. Heat a little oil in a pan over a medium heat, add the chorizo and fry until golden. Add the diced pepper and continue to sauté. Add a splash each of red wine and balsamic vinegar, then add the parsley, season to taste and set aside.

Heat a little oil in a small frying pan and cook the scallops for I to 2 minutes on each side, or until they have a golden crust. Deglaze the pan with the lemon juice and tip the cooking juices into the chorizo pan. Arrange the chorizo mixture in a small line on each serving plate, top with an equal amount of scallops and serve immediately.

JAMIE OLIVER

Smoked mackerel & roast potato salad

SERVES
4

- 750g new potatoes, larger ones halved
- olive oil
- 1 tablespoon coriander seeds
- 2 lemons
- sea salt and freshly ground black pepper
- 4 garlic cloves
- extra virgin olive oil
- 4 smoked mackerel fillets
- 2 handfuls of watercress, washed and spun dry
- bunch of spring onions, trimmed and finely sliced
- handful of mixed cress, to serve

Preheat the oven to 200°C/400°F/gas 6. Bring a large pan of salted water to the boil. Parboil your potatoes for about 5 to 6 minutes, drain, then allow to steam dry. Transfer to a roasting tray, crush them lightly and drizzle with a good lug of olive oil.

Crush the coriander seeds in a pestle and mortar, and peel in thick strips of zest from 1 of your lemons. Add to the potatoes, season well, then add the juice from 1 lemon and the unpeeled garlic cloves. Toss it all together, then roast for 30 minutes, or until the potatoes are golden and crispy. Remove from the oven and leave to cool for a few minutes.

Meanwhile, mix the juice of half the remaining lemon with three times as much extra virgin olive oil in a large bowl, season well and set aside.

Scatter the cooled potatoes over a large platter, then flake over your smoked mackerel with a fork. Add the watercress and spring onions to the bowl with the lemon dressing and toss quickly until lightly coated. Scatter this on top of the fish and potatoes, sprinkle with the mixed cress, then serve with some fresh crusty bread.

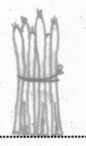

Recipe © Jamie Oliver. Portrait © David Loftus.

THEO RANDALL

Pan-fried squid with borlotti beans

For the beans
- 300g dried borlotti beans
- I sprig of fresh sage
- I fresh red chilli, pricked with a knife
- I garlic clove, peeled and quartered
- 2 tomatoes
- sea salt and freshly ground black pepper
- 3 tablespoons olive oil
- I teaspoon red wine vinegar

For the squid
- 6 whole fresh squid
- extra virgin olive oil
- I fresh red chilli, deseeded and finely chopped
- 3 anchovy fillets, chopped
- bunch of fresh flat-leaf parsley, leaves picked and chopped
- juice of ½ lemon, plus extra to serve
- 2 large handfuls of rocket, washed, spun dry and chopped, to serve

Soak the beans overnight in plenty of cold water.

The next day, drain the beans and transfer to a large pan with three times the quantity of water. Add the sage, chilli, garlic and tomatoes. Bring to the boil, then reduce to a gentle simmer for I hour, or until the beans are tender (cooking times will vary depending on the age of the beans).

Drain and discard three-quarters of the cooking liquor, then transfer the beans and remaining liquor to a bowl, discarding the sage, chilli and tomatoes. Remove the garlic, mash it with a fork, then stir it back into the beans. Season to taste, then stir in the olive oil and red wine vinegar and set aside.

For the squid, peel off the wings and outer membranes and remove the heads and intestines. Cut them in half lengthways and scrape out the insides with a knife. Wash thoroughly with cold water and pat dry. Lay the squid, skin-side down, and score with a criss-cross pattern. Season and rub a little extra virgin olive oil into the skin. Place a large non-stick pan over a medium heat. When hot, add the squid, scored-side down (you may need to do this in two batches), cook for I minute until golden, then turn over.

Add the chilli, anchovies, parsley and lemon juice to the pan. Remove the squid and quickly slice it into bite-sized pieces, then immediately return it to the pan and toss briefly with the other ingredients. To serve, spoon some of the borlotti beans in the centre of a plate. Dress the rocket leaves with lemon juice and extra virgin olive oil, then place on top of the beans, followed by the pan-fried squid.

WAHACA
THOMASINA MIERS

These Oaxacan-style pizzas, known as "tlayudas" in Mexico, are delicious and wonderfully messy to eat. They are usually sold at night-time to people coming out of bars in Oaxaca. You can fill them with just about anything you like, from grilled chorizo and skirt steak to fish and seasonal vegetables.

Oaxacan-style pizzas

SERVES
4

- I large bag of baby spinach (roughly 400g)
- small knob of butter
- sea salt and freshly ground black pepper
- olive oil
- 2 large flatbreads
- I to 2 fresh green chillies
- I ripe Hass avocado
- 125g ball of mozzarella
- 80g pecorino or mature Cheddar, grated
- 200g shredded leftover cooked free-range chicken
- 8 sun-blushed tomatoes or 2 very ripe fresh tomatoes, sliced
- ½ small bunch of soft fresh herbs (basil, tarragon, chervil or coriander), leaves picked and roughly chopped
- 2 handfuls of rocket, washed and spun dry

Wash the spinach in cold water and shake dry. Heat a large pan over a medium heat, add the butter, then the spinach and cook for a few minutes until the spinach has wilted down a little. Remove the spinach from the pan, squeeze dry and season to taste, adding a little drizzle of oil, then set aside.

Heat a frying or flat griddle pan large enough to hold the flatbreads. Put the chillies on the pan and cook for about 10 minutes, turning frequently, until they are blistered and charred all over. Roughly chop and set aside.

Put the pan back on the heat, add one flatbread, sprinkle with a little water and gently heat through. Once slightly crisp, turn over. Cut open the avocado, scoop out the flesh of one half with a spoon and dot it over the flatbread. Tear over half of the mozzarella, and scatter with half of the remaining ingredients (including the wilted spinach and the chopped chilli). When the outside of the flatbread is crisp and the mozzarella has begun to melt, fold it over so it looks like an open calzone. Slide it onto a serving plate and slice into pieces. Repeat with the remaining flatbread and ingredients.

PS. To complete your Mexican experience, serve with hot, freshly made salsas, some wedges of lime and a couple of cold beers!

Recipe taken from *Mexican Food Made Simple* by Thomasina Miers (Hodder & Stoughton, £20). Portrait © Tara Fisher

FIFTEEN
ANDREW PARKINSON

This tasty wrap is a good mix of carbs, protein and veggies. It's the perfect snack for festivals and outdoor celebrations when you need all the balanced energy you can get.

Chicken, guacamole & salad wraps

- I small free-range cooked, smoked chicken (roughly I.4kg), available from the butcher's
- 8 wholemeal tortillas

For the guacamole
- 4 ripe avocados
- I fresh red chilli, deseeded
- I small red onion, peeled
- I small garlic clove
- small bunch of fresh coriander
- sea salt and freshly ground black pepper
- juice of 2 limes
- Worcestershire sauce

For the salad
- 2 large ripe tomatoes
- I red onion, peeled
- 2 garlic cloves, peeled
- I fennel bulb, trimmed
- I fresh red chilli
- 2 baby gem lettuces
- juice of I lemon
- extra virgin olive oil

Pick all of the chicken meat, discarding the bones, then shred and set aside.

For the guacamole, halve the avocados, remove the stones, then scoop the flesh into a bowl. Finely chop the chilli, onion, garlic and coriander (including the stalks). Add to the avocado bowl and mash together with a fork. Season to taste with salt and pepper, lime juice and a splash of Worcestershire sauce.

For the salad, dice the tomatoes, then finely slice the onion, garlic, fennel and chilli. Shred the lettuces, then wash in cold water and spin-dry well. Toss together, season to taste, add the lemon juice and a good drizzle of oil and mix well.

To serve, fold the tortillas like pouches and start to build your wraps. Simply stuff a little salad, smoked chicken and guacamole into each, and use leftovers to make more.

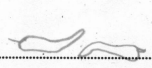

Recipe © Andrew Parkinson. Portrait © Hoi Ling Mak

BENARES
ATUL KOCHHAR

Chicken tikka pie

1kg free-range corn-fed skinless, boneless chicken thighs, cut into 4cm chunks

For the first marinade
- 1 garlic clove, peeled
- 1cm piece of fresh ginger, peeled
- 1 teaspoon chilli powder
- juice of ½ lemon

For the second marinade
- 250g Greek-style yoghurt
- 1 teaspoon each garam masala and ground coriander
- 50ml vegetable oil
- ½ teaspoon each ground cinnamon, chilli powder and dried fenugreek leaves
- 2 teaspoons gram flour

For brushing
- small knob of butter
- 2 teaspoons lime juice
- 1 teaspoon chaat masala or garam masala

For the pastry
- 250g plain flour, plus extra for dusting
- 1 teaspoon sea salt
- 250g cold unsalted butter

For the masala
- 1 small onion, peeled
- 10 garlic cloves, peeled
- vegetable oil
- 6cm piece of fresh ginger, peeled
- 3 level teaspoons each ground coriander, chilli powder, turmeric and garam masala
- 2 large bunches of fresh coriander, leaves picked
- 3 ripe tomatoes

For the first marinade, finely grate the garlic and ginger and place in a bowl. Add the chilli powder, lemon juice and chicken, then set aside to marinate for 30 minutes. For the second marinade, add all of the ingredients to the chicken bowl, mix together well, then leave to marinate for a further 4 to 6 hours. Skewer the marinated chicken pieces and cook over a barbecue, or in a hot oven at 200°C/400°F/ gas 6, for 15 minutes, or until cooked through. Brush with a mixture of butter, lime juice and chaat masala and set aside.

For the pastry, sieve the flour and salt into a bowl. Cube the butter, then rub in with your fingertips until the mixture resembles breadcrumbs. Add 105ml of cold water and gently mix into dough. Dust the dough with flour, wrap in cling film and leave to rest in the fridge for 30 minutes.

Preheat the oven to 160°C/325°F/gas 3. For the masala, chop the onion and garlic, then add with a little vegetable oil to a pan over a medium heat and sauté for 5 minutes until soft. Finely grate the ginger into the pan and cook for 2 minutes until golden. Stir through the spices, then chop the coriander and tomatoes and add to the pan, stirring to combine. Stir for a couple more minutes until everything is cooked through. Toss the chicken in the masala. Roll out the pastry to just under ½cm thick. Line the base of a pie dish (roughly 20cm x 20cm x 6cm), then add the chicken filling. Lay another piece of pastry on top, seal the edges, trim off any excess and poke a small hole in the top. Bake in the oven for 35 to 40 minutes, or until the pastry is golden and the filling is piping hot.

Recipe © Atul Kochhar

CANTEEN

The tradition of potting, preserving meat or fish in a pot sealed with a layer of fat, has a very long history in this country. Our potted duck has a deep savoury flavour and we think it makes a good meal for sharing, with plenty of toast and a bit of home-made piccalilli.

Potted duck with piccalilli & toast

SERVES 6

- 4 good-quality duck legs, preferably Gressingham duck
- sea salt and freshly ground black pepper
- I garlic bulb
- 3 sprigs of fresh sage, leaves picked and chopped
- 3 fresh bay leaves
- 100ml pale ale
- 2 tablespoons Madeira
- big pinch of ground mace
- home-made piccalilli, to serve
- 12 slices of brown bread, toasted, to serve

Preheat the oven to 110°C/225°F/gas ¼. Sprinkle the duck legs with I teaspoon of salt and place in a casserole dish with a close-fitting lid. Separate the garlic bulb into cloves. Bash the cloves with the back of a knife, then peel them and add to the duck casserole with the sage, bay leaves and ale. Cover and cook in the oven for 4 to 5 hours, or until the meat is tender and falling off the bone.

Drain the duck and reserve the cooking liquor (including the duck fat); keep the garlic and discard the bay leaves. When the meat is cool enough to handle, discard the skin and bones and shred the meat with your fingers into a bowl. Squash the garlic cloves and add to the shredded meat. Add the Madeira, mace and lots of pepper. Reserve a few tablespoons of the duck fat, then slowly beat the remaining fat and cooking

liquor into the meat until it is all incorporated and looks creamy. Season to taste and pack into an earthenware dish (roughly 750ml capacity).

Pour the reserved duck fat over the top, then chill in the fridge for at least 6 hours. Remove from the fridge half an hour before eating. Serve with home-made piccalilli and toast. The leftover potted duck will keep, refrigerated, for up to one week.

PALE ALE

Recipe © www.canteen.co.uk

THE PROVIDORES
PETER GORDON

Eating outdoors is all about enjoying the sociable chaos of happy crowds and savouring the heightened flavours of your food, so make sure you pack plenty of delicious chutneys, pickles and spices in your basket. Make everything ahead of time and assemble at your picnic location.

NZ lamb Sam with gooseberry chutney

SERVES 10

- I boned leg of New Zealand lamb, cut into 3 muscles (roughly Ikg boned weight); get your butcher to do this for you
- I tablespoon each cumin seeds, coriander seeds and dried red chilli flakes, plus extra for seasoning
- I0cm stick of cinnamon
- 2 tablespoons sesame seeds
- 50ml olive oil
- sea salt
- 2 red onions, peeled
- 4 garlic cloves, peeled
- 200g unrefined caster sugar
- 400ml tin of chopped tomatoes
- 200g fresh or frozen gooseberries
- 50ml tamarind paste
- ½ bunch of fresh mint
- 200ml Greek-style yoghurt
- I0 burger buns or ciabatta rolls
- 2 large handfuls of salad leaves, washed and spun dry

Trim the lamb of excess fat. Toast the cumin and coriander seeds in a pan over a medium heat for a couple of minutes, then roughly grind with the chilli flakes and cinnamon in a pestle and mortar. Mix half of the crushed spices (reserve remaining) with the sesame seeds, 25ml of the oil and a good pinch of salt. Rub this all over the lamb, then leave it to marinate for 3 to 8 hours.

Meanwhile, slice the onions and garlic and sauté them in the remaining oil on a low-medium heat for about 10 minutes, or until caramelised. Add the remaining crushed spices and the sugar and bring to a bubble. Add the tomatoes, gooseberries and tamarind paste and bring to the boil, then reduce the heat and cook over a rapid simmer until the chutney thickens, stirring frequently to prevent it sticking to the pan. Season to taste with salt and extra chilli flakes, if needed.

Pick and shred the mint leaves into a bowl, then mix in the yoghurt and set aside. Preheat the oven to 170°C, or crank up the barbecue. Cook the lamb for about 30 to 40 minutes, or until cooked medium. Let it rest for 10 minutes before slicing.

Spread the chutney over the bottom bun halves, then add the salad leaves, sliced lamb, yoghurt and bun tops.

Recipe © The Providores - Peter Gordon. Portrait © Jonathan Gregson

GOURMET BURGER KITCHEN
TIM MOLEMA

Minted lamb burgers with feta & tomato jam

For the tomato jam
- 750g mixed beef and plum tomatoes
- 1 star anise
- ½ teaspoon each black peppercorns, coriander seeds and juniper berries
- 2 cardamom pods
- 2 cloves
- 100g caster sugar
- ½ teaspoon vanilla extract
- zest and juice of 1 orange and 1 lemon
- 1 teaspoon sea salt

For the burgers
- 1kg good-quality minced lamb
- 3 to 4 shallots, peeled and very finely chopped
- 2 garlic cloves, peeled and crushed
- 1 teaspoon ground cumin
- ½ teaspoon dried mint
- 10g fresh mint leaves, chopped
- ½ teaspoon ground black pepper
- 1 teaspoon sea salt

For the cheat's aioli
- 100g mayonnaise, made from free-range eggs
- 2 garlic cloves, peeled and crushed, or to taste

To assemble
- 6 good-quality large burger buns
- 50g feta
- English lettuce leaves and a few very thin red onion rings

For the tomato jam, halve the tomatoes, scrape out the seeds, roughly chop the flesh and add to a heavy-based non-stick pan. Toast all the spices in a separate frying pan over a medium heat until fragrant. Cool, then grind in a pestle and mortar and add to the tomato pan along with the sugar, vanilla extract, lemon and orange zest, juices and salt. Warm over a low heat until the sugar dissolves, then cook over a medium heat, stirring regularly, for 45 minutes to 1 hour, or until the jam coats the back of a wooden spoon. (Don't let the jam burn; if it's bubbling too much, turn the heat down.) Remove from the heat, add more salt, if needed, and cool. The jam will keep, refrigerated, for 2 to 3 weeks, or you can preserve it for longer in sterilised jars.

For the burgers, place all the ingredients in a large bowl and mix together by hand until just combined. Shape the mixture into 6 patties (roughly 10cm wide and 2½cm thick). Cook over a high heat in a frying or a griddle pan, or over a barbecue, for about 4 minutes on each side, turning every 2 minutes. Meanwhile, mix the mayonnaise with the crushed garlic, adding more garlic to taste.

To assemble, lightly toast the burger buns. Spread a little aioli on the bottom bun halves, add a burger patty, then crumble over or add a thin slice of feta. Top with a good dollop of tomato jam, some lettuce leaves and onion rings, then finish with the bun tops. Eat and go to heaven (or play Frisbee).

PS. For helpful hints on how to sterilise jam jars, go to page 50.

BARBECOA
ADAM PERRY LANG
& JAMIE OLIVER

Dry-aged rump steaks with charred aubergine

- 4 good-quality dry-aged rump steaks (roughly 200g each)
- large handful of wild rocket, washed and spun dry

For the aubergine
- 1 large aubergine (roughly 500g)
- 300g vine-ripened cherry tomatoes
- 50ml olive oil, plus extra for drizzling
- sea salt and freshly ground black pepper
- 1 fresh red chilli
- 2 sprigs of fresh marjoram
- 1 long shallot, peeled
- juice of 1 lemon

For the lemon vinaigrette
- juice of ½ lemon
- 1 teaspoon runny honey
- 3 tablespoons extra virgin olive oil
- white pepper

For the lemon yoghurt
- juice of ½ lemon
- 4 tablespoons natural yoghurt

For the aubergine, preheat your oven to 180ºC/350ºF/gas 4. Cook the whole aubergine in a dry pan or over the flame on your gas hob for 10 minutes, turning with tongs, until blackened and blistered all over. When cool enough to handle, peel and discard the skin, then set aside. Drizzle the tomatoes with a little olive oil on a roasting tray and season well. Roast them in the oven for 15 minutes, or until soft. Meanwhile, finely chop the chilli, marjoram and shallot. Add to a bowl with the roasted tomatoes, charred aubergine, lemon juice and 50ml olive oil. Mix well, season to taste and set aside.

For the lemon vinaigrette, mix all of the ingredients together in a small bowl, then season to taste with salt and white pepper, set aside. Repeat in a separate bowl with the ingredients for the lemon yoghurt.

Preheat a griddle pan on a high heat. Season the steaks, drizzle with olive oil, then cook for 2 minutes on each side for medium rare, or longer if you prefer it well done. Once cooked, let the steaks rest for a couple of minutes, then trim off most of the fat. Meanwhile, warm the charred aubergine in a small pan over a low heat.

Divide the charred aubergine between serving plates. Drizzle with a little lemon yoghurt and top with a steak. Quickly dress the rocket in the lemon vinaigrette, then place the leaves around the meat. Sprinkle with a little extra salt and pepper, then serve immediately.

Recipe © Barbecoa. Portrait © David Loftus

Braised pork, leek, mushroom & cider pie

SERVES
6

- 1kg good-quality pork shoulder
- sea salt and freshly ground black pepper
- plain flour, for dusting
- rapeseed oil
- 50g unsalted butter
- 500g leeks, trimmed and diced
- 400g small chestnut mushrooms, washed and roughly chopped
- 2 fresh bay leaves
- 30g tomato purée
- 10g garlic purée
- 1 litre Magners cider
- 2 organic chicken stock cubes
- 10g fresh tarragon, leaves picked
- 20g Dijon mustard
- 250g ready-made puff pastry
- 1 large free-range or organic egg, beaten, for brushing

Preheat your oven to 160ºC/325ºF/ gas 3. Remove and discard the layer of fat around the pork shoulder, then cut the meat into 3cm dice. Season and dust lightly with flour. Add with a good lug of rapeseed oil to a pan over a high heat and seal, tossing occasionally, for about 10 minutes, or until the pork is evenly coloured. Add the butter, leeks, mushrooms, bay leaves, tomato and garlic purées. Cook for 5 minutes, stirring frequently, then add the cider. Bring to a simmer, then crumble in the stock cubes and mix well (add a little more hot water, if needed). Stir through the tarragon and mustard, then cover with a lid and braise in the oven for 2 hours, or until the meat pulls apart. (If it needs a little longer, pop it back in the oven until the meat is tender). If your sauce is too thin, transfer the pan to your hob and let it bubble away over a high heat until the sauce has thickened. When it's ready, season to taste and let it cool.

Turn the oven up to 190ºC/375ºF/gas 5. Transfer the pork filling to a pie dish (roughly 20cm x 20cm x 6cm deep). Roll out the pastry until just under ½cm thick. Place over the pie dish, leaving 2cm of pastry to overhang, fold over the edges, crimp to seal and brush with the egg wash. Poke a small hole in the top and bake in the oven for about 30 minutes, or until the pastry is golden and the filling is piping hot.

Recipe © Andrew Parkinson. Portrait © Hoi Ling Mak

CIDER

JO PRATT

This is the perfect breakfast dish to keep you going until lunch and beyond. It's easy enough to cook outdoors too; all you need is a campfire or stove and a trusty frying pan.

Sweet potato hash browns with sausages

- 2 to 3 tablespoons olive oil
- 4 good-quality sausages (whatever flavour you fancy)
- 150g peeled sweet potato
- 1 large free-range or organic egg, beaten
- sea salt and freshly ground black pepper
- 200g cherry tomatoes
- 1 teaspoon caster sugar
- 1 teaspoon balsamic vinegar
- pinch of dried chilli flakes
- 2 sprigs of fresh flat-leaf parsley, chopped, to serve

Heat 1 tablespoon of oil in a medium to large non-stick frying pan. Cut the sausages, on an angle, into 1 to 2cm-thick slices, add to the pan and cook over a high heat for about 5 minutes, or until cooked through and turning golden, then remove from the pan and keep warm.

Coarsely grate the sweet potato into a bowl. Mix in the egg and season well. Divide into four patties. If there isn't much oil left in the pan, add a tablespoon more. Once hot, add the hash browns to the pan, flatten each one slightly with a spoon and cook over a medium heat for 2 to 3 minutes on each side, or until golden and crispy.

Meanwhile, heat the remaining tablespoon of oil in a separate small frying pan. Add the tomatoes and cook over a medium heat until they begin to soften. Add the sugar, balsamic vinegar and chilli flakes and season well. Cook for a couple of minutes until the tomatoes are squishy.

To serve, place two hash browns on each plate, top with the sausages and tomatoes, then sprinkle with the parsley.

PS. If you're in the mood for something a bit more sophisticated, you could top the hash browns with cooked asparagus, poached eggs and some crème fraîche mixed with fresh chives and lemon juice.

Recipe © Jo Pratt

LOCANDA LOCATELLI
GIORGIO LOCATELLI

These flatbreads, or "piadine", remind me of my childhood. I used to eat them as street food when my grandparents took me on holiday to Romagna. The perfect fillings are ham and squacquerone, which comes from the Ferrara region, but, in reality, any soft cheese will do.

Italian-style flatbreads

MAKES
8-10

For the dough
- 65g unsalted butter
- 500g Tipo "00" flour, plus extra for dusting
- 1 heaped tablespoon baking powder
- 1 level tablespoon sea salt
- 275ml milk

For the filling
- 70g rocket, washed and spun dry
- extra virgin olive oil
- 350g burrata or squacquerone, available from your local Italian deli
- 10 slices of Parma ham

For the dough, melt the butter in a small pan over a low heat, then leave to cool a little. Meanwhile, mix the flour, baking powder and salt in a large bowl, then gradually add the milk and the cooled melted butter. Stir together, then cover the bowl with cling film and let the mixture rest for half an hour.

Roll the dough out on a flour-dusted surface until ½cm thick. Cut out 15cm-diameter rounds, then roll each one out a little wider until about 1 to 2mm thick. Let the flatbreads rest for 20 minutes.

Warm up a large non-stick pan over a medium heat, and cook the flatbreads, one at at time, for about 1 to 2 minutes on each side, or until golden. Set aside.

For the filling, toss the rocket in a bowl with a little oil and set aside. If using burrata, chop or mash it until you've got a spreadable consistency. Spread a bit of the burrata or squacquerone on each flatbread, tear over a slice of ham and add a small handful of dressed rocket. Serve them flat on the plate, then get your guests to fold them over to eat.

BURRATA

WAHACA THOMASINA MIERS

Quesadillas are perfect for sharing. Crispy and oozing with melted cheese, and anything else you fancy, they can be enjoyed at any time of day. Make a few fillings and salsas, grate some cheese and rustle up a salad, then let everyone make their own. Simply slice them up and eat them hot.

Chorizo, potato & thyme quesadillas

SERVES 6

- 350g potatoes
- sea salt and freshly ground black pepper
- olive oil
- ½ onion, peeled and finely chopped
- small bunch of fresh thyme, leaves picked and shredded
- 200g good-quality cooking chorizo, chopped
- I garlic clove, peeled and chopped
- 6 large flour or corn tortillas
- 150g freshly grated extra mature Cheddar
- 125g ball of mozzarella

Peel the potatoes and cut them into 2cm chunks. Add them to a pan of salted boiling water and cook until they are soft but still hold their shape. Drain and leave to steam dry.

Heat a large frying pan over a medium heat. When hot, add a tablespoon of oil, then wait a minute before adding the onion, thyme and chorizo. Cook for about 10 minutes, or until the onion is soft and the chorizo is cooked through. Season well, add the garlic and cook for a further 3 minutes. Add the boiled potato, turn up the heat and fry everything for another 5 minutes until the potato absorbs all the flavours. Season to taste.

Divide the chorizo mixture between the tortillas, spreading it onto half of each one. Sprinkle with the grated Cheddar and tear over pieces of mozzarella.

Fold each tortilla over, brush with a little oil and cook, one or two at a time, in a hot, dry frying or griddle pan until golden and crisp. Cut into wedges and serve with your favourite fresh salsa.

Recipe taken from *Mexican Food Made Simple* by Thomasina Miers (Hodder & Stoughton, £20). Portrait © Tara Fisher

THE WOMEN'S INSTITUTE

Easy-peasy strawberry jam

- lkg jam sugar with pectin (not preserving sugar)
- 2kg strawberries
- juice of ½ lemon

Pop a couple of saucers in the freezer before you start. Pour the sugar into a large thick-bottomed pan. Pick through the strawberries, discarding any blemished fruit, then hull the remaining. Add the hulled strawberries and lemon juice to the pan, stir gently, then leave for 1 hour.

Put the pan over a medium heat, bring to the boil and boil rapidly for 30 to 40 minutes, skimming off any scum as it appears. Remove from the heat and test the setting point: take a saucer from the freezer, drop a small spoonful of jam on to it and allow it to cool for a minute. Push your finger through the jam – if it drags, it's ready; if not, boil the jam for a few more minutes, and continue to test it as above until the setting point has been reached.

When the jam is ready, turn off the heat and leave it to stand for 15 to 20 minutes. Pour into sterilised jars, seal tightly with screw-top lids while still hot and label.

PS. There are a couple of golden rules for making jams, jellies and marmalades:

- Use dry, unblemished fruit that is not overripe.

- All equipment must be scrupulously clean and your jars and lids must be sterilised. If you have a dishwasher, put them through a high-heat cycle (or wash and rinse them well in hot water), then place them on a baking tray and slide it into a hot oven (160°C/325°F/gas 3) for 10 to 15 minutes. Keep them warm until you pour in the jam. Always seal jams while hot.

VINOTECA JOHN MURRAY

Creamy dark chocolate with English raspberries

SERVES 8

For the creamy dark chocolate
- 3 large free-range or organic egg yolks
- 25g Demerara sugar
- 200ml double cream
- 150g good-quality dark chocolate (70% cocoa solids), broken up

For the chocolate crumble
- 40g Demerara sugar
- 40g unsalted butter
- 40g ground almonds
- 35g plain flour
- 1 teaspoon cocoa powder

For the coconut crunch
- 50g caster sugar
- 30g unsalted butter
- pinch of sea salt
- splash of milk
- 30g desiccated coconut
- 1 tablespoon plain flour

For the raspberry ganache
- 100g English raspberries
- 100g good-quality white chocolate, broken up

To assemble
- 2 tablespoons flaked almonds, toasted
- 1 punnet of English raspberries
- cocoa powder

For the creamy dark chocolate, whisk the yolks and sugar together in a bowl. Pour the double cream into a pan and bring to the boil, then remove from the heat. Pour a small amount of boiling cream into the yolk mixture and stir to combine, then add the tempered yolk mixture to the cream in the pan. Return the pan to the hob and cook gently over a low heat until it reaches a light custard consistency. Pour this over the broken dark chocolate, placed in a bowl, and stir until melted and combined. Pop the chocolate mixture into the fridge to cool. Bring it out 1 hour before serving (it should have a consistency like peanut butter).

For the chocolate crumble, cream the sugar and butter in a bowl until light and fluffy. Fold in the remaining ingredients until just combined. Roll the mixture into a log, wrap it in cling film and freeze for at least 30 minutes. When ready to serve, grate the crumble onto a baking tray, lined with parchment paper, and cook at 160ºC/325ºF/gas 3 for 8 to 12 minutes, then let it cool.

For the coconut crunch, preheat the oven to 150ºC/300ºF/ gas 2. Cream the sugar, butter and salt in a bowl until light and fluffy. Stir in the milk, then fold through the coconut and flour. Rest in the fridge for 30 minutes, then spread out dessertspoonfuls of the mixture on a baking tray, lined with parchment paper, until 3mm thick. Bake for 9 to 15 minutes, or until golden, set aside.

For the raspberry ganache, mash the raspberries through a sieve into a pan. Bring to the boil, then pour the raspberries over the white chocolate, placed in a bowl, and stir until melted and combined. Keep refrigerated.

To assemble, spoon some raspberry ganache into each serving bowl and sprinkle with chocolate crumble. Warm a spoon in boiling water and use it to add a quenelle of creamy dark chocolate. Add two shards of coconut crunch, a sprinkling of almonds, a few fresh raspberries and a dusting of cocoa powder, then serve immediately.

Recipe © Vinoteca – John Murray

THE SHOREDITCH SISTERS

For a refreshing treat, cut up fruit such as oranges, limes and lemons, or strawberries and raspberries, and place them in ice-cube trays or yoghurt pots filled with water. Freeze them overnight, then pack in your cool box along with your favourite tipple. This is a lovely way to enjoy iced drinks in the sun.

Apple & custard cake

Recipe © The Shoreditch Sisters. Portrait © Peter Schiazza

SERVES 6

- 100g unsalted butter, at room temperature, plus extra for greasing
- 100g caster sugar
- 2 large free-range or organic eggs, beaten
- 175g self-raising flour
- pinch of sea salt
- 1 teaspoon ground cinnamon
- 1 large cooking apple, such as Bramley, peeled
- ½ an eating apple, such as English cox
- splash of milk, if needed

For the custard icing
- 75ml milk
- 70g caster sugar
- 1 teaspoon vanilla extract
- 1 large free-range or organic egg yolk, beaten
- 1 tablespoon cornflour, mixed into a paste with a little water
- 90g butter unsalted butter, at room temperature
- ground cinnamon, for dusting

Preheat the oven to 180°C/350°F/gas 4. Grease an 18cm loose-bottomed cake tin with butter. Cream the butter and sugar together in a large bowl, then beat in the eggs. Sift in and fold through the flour, salt and cinnamon. Cut the cooking apple into small cubes; coarsely grate the eating apple. Stir both into the cake mixture. If needed, add a splash of milk (the mixture should have a dropping consistency).

Spoon the cake mixture into the prepared tin. Bake in the oven for about 40 minutes, or until golden and cooked through. To check, insert a skewer into the centre of the cake; if it comes out clean, it's ready. Leave it to cool a little in the tin, then transfer it to a wire rack to cool completely. (You can also make cupcakes with this recipe; divide the mixture among 16 cupcake cases and bake for 15 to 20 minutes).

For the custard icing, heat the milk, sugar and vanilla extract in a small saucepan over a medium heat until just boiling. Whisk a tiny bit of the hot milk into the egg yolk, gradually adding a little at a time until you've added half. Return the egg yolk mixture to the milk, whisking constantly. Whisk for about 5 minutes over a low heat, or until you get a light coating consistency. Gradually whisk in the cornflour paste until the mixture thickens, then pour into a small bowl, cover with cling film and pop in the fridge for 1 hour.

Beat the butter in a bowl until almost whipped, then gradually add the cooled custard to the butter. Spread onto your cake (or cupcakes) and dust with a little cinnamon before serving.

THE PROVIDORES
PETER GORDON

According to my paternal grandmother Molly, the wheat-free crunchy and slightly crumbly slice that I based this recipe on was my Dad's favourite as a young man. Why it's associated with Sydney is anyone's guess – we have no relative called Sydney, and Dad didn't go to Australia until I was 16 years old!

Brazil nut & goji berry Sydney special

MAKES 12-20

- 180g unsalted butter
- 200g light muscovado or light brown sugar
- 30g goji berries (you could also use dried cranberries or sultanas)
- 170g oatmeal or rolled oats
- 80g desiccated coconut
- 70g Brazil nuts, chopped
- pinch of sea salt

Preheat your oven to 160°C/325°F/gas 3. Line a 25cm square baking tin with parchment paper.

Melt the butter in a saucepan over a low-medium heat. Stir in the sugar and berries and keep stirring, turning the heat up slightly, until the sugar has melted into the butter (it should look like a fatty caramel). Mix in the remaining ingredients, then gently press the mixture into the tin.

Bake in the centre of the oven for 15 to 20 minutes, turning the tin about halfway through, until dark golden. Leave to cool for 5 minutes, then use a bread knife to cut it into slices while still in the tin (you can get 12 or 20 slices, depending on how large you want to cut them). Leave them to cool in the tin, then carefully remove and place on a wire rack for 10 minutes. The slices will keep, in an airtight container, for up to one week.

Recipe taken from *Fusion: A Culinary Journey* by Peter Gordon (Jacqui Small). Portrait © Jonathan Gregson

RACHEL ALLEN

Peanut butter & white chocolate blondies

MAKES
12-16

- 100g butter, at room temperature, plus extra for greasing
- 125g plain flour
- 1 teaspoon baking powder
- 150g crunchy peanut butter
- 175g light brown sugar
- 1 large free-range or organic egg, beaten
- 1 teaspoon vanilla extract
- 75g good-quality white chocolate, chopped

Preheat the oven to 170°C. Butter the sides of a 20cm square cake tin and line the base with parchment paper.

Sift the flour and baking powder into a small bowl and set aside. Cream the butter and peanut butter together in a large bowl until very soft. Add the sugar, egg and vanilla extract and beat until well combined. Add the sifted flour mixture and the chopped chocolate and mix to form a dough.

Press the dough into the prepared tin in a fairly even layer and bake in the oven for 25 to 30 minutes, or until golden and almost firm in the centre. Remove from the oven and allow to cool in the tin, before removing and cutting into squares.

Recipe © Rachel Allen

Flavoured
waters

When you're out in the sun all day, it's important to stay hydrated. Fortunately, it only takes a few seconds to turn a plain jug of water into something much more exciting.

Chuck a few handfuls of ice into a jug or large bottle, add any one of these simple flavour combos and top up with still or sparkling water:

- Go classic with a few slices of fresh lemon or lime.

- Quarter an orange, squeeze in all of the juice, then toss in the squeezed quarters for colour and extra flavour.

- Mash up a handful of strawberries or raspberries with a fork, then add to the jug and stir through.

- Scrunch a handful of fresh mint in your hands to get the flavour going, then add that to the jug with a squeeze of lemon or lime juice. If you're feeling a bit adventurous, add a few slices of cucumber too.

- Halve a pomegranate and, holding it cut-side down in your hand, bash it with the back of a spoon so that all of the seeds come tumbling out. Add a few mint leaves and stir well.

Committee chefs and restaurateurs at The Big Feastival

LOCANDA LOCATELLI – GIORGIO LOCATELLI

In a few short years, Locanda Locatelli, the creation of husband-and wife team Giorgio and Plaxy Locatelli, has become a formidable landmark on London's fine-dining scene. Since February 2002, the restaurant has been awarded a Michelin star in recognition of the exquisite Italian dishes that Giorgio creates in the kitchen. www.locandalocatelli.com

THE PROVIDORES – PETER GORDON

Peter Gordon and Michael McGrath's The Providores brings the finest in fusion food to the heart of London's Marylebone Village. The all-day café and wine bar downstairs and the formal dining room upstairs feature ever-changing menus that are driven by creativity, innovation and the use of prime ingredients, both from within the UK and abroad. www.theprovidores.co.uk

REDHOOK – JONATHAN DOWNEY

Specialising in seafood and steaks, Redhook brings surf-and-turf heaven to Farringdon. At the heart of the restaurant is an oyster bar and charocal oven and an extenstive wine list, which features more than 70 great wines from the Americas, plus a few favourite clarets, not to mention the killer cocktails you'd expect from the owners of Milk & Honey. www.redhooklondon.com

WAHACA – THOMASINA MIERS

Thomasina Miers brings the vibrant food of Mexico to the UK with her chain of London restaurants, inspired by her travels through Mexico and the country's fantastic markets and street stalls. Wahaca has become a popular choice for diners in search of a lively atmosphere and a mouth-watering selection of dishes that are perfect for sharing at any time of day. www.wahaca.co.uk

Restaurants at The Big Feastival

BARBECOA – ADAM PERRY LANG & JAMIE OLIVER

Adam Perry Lang and Jamie Oliver have drawn on traditional cooking techniques from around the world to create a celebration of the relationship between fire and food at Barbecoa. Combined with its open kitchen and spectacular views of St Paul's Cathedral, Barbecoa has become a foodie destination right in the heart of London. www.barbecoa.com

BENARES – ATUL KOCHHAR

Benares has established itself as one of the finest Michelin-starred restaurants in London. The spectacularly modern dishes created by chef Atul Kochhar are matched only by the restaurant's sophisticated setting. Atul has been celebrated for reinventing Indian cuisine and changing the way people perceive and experience Indian food. www.benaresrestaurant.com

CAFÉ SPICE NAMASTÉ– PERVIN & CYRUS TODIWALA

Cyrus and Pervin Todiwala, the dynamic team behind Café Spice Namasté, have created a landmark Indian restaurant inspired by the culinary riches of their Parsee heritage. The restaurant is renowned the world over for chef Cyrus's ability to meld exotic flavours and spices, creating unusual twists on traditional dishes. Winner of the 2011 Sustainable Food Award. www.cafespice.co.uk

CANTEEN

GREAT BRITISH FOOD

Canteen took the London restaurant scene by storm in 2005 and now the chain has established itself as a champion of proper British food, focusing on provenance with pride and passion. Canteen's no-nonsense, modern-meets-classic menu, served in an informal setting, has won it legions of fans on the high street and brought widespread critical acclaim. www.canteen.co.uk

Restaurants at The Big Feastival

FIFTEEN – ANDREW PARKINSON

Since 2002, Fifteen has been offering its Apprentice Programme for young people in need of a break, while serving fresh seasonal menus of gorgeous Italian-inspired food. Head chef Andrew Parkinson has been running the kitchen at Fifteen London for six years, leading the team of professional chefs and training apprentices. www.fifteen.net

GOURMET BURGER KITCHEN – TIM MOLEMA

GBK is all about the burgers. The highest-quality meats, freshest home-made sauces and artisan buns have made the chain's cooked-to-order creations a popular choice among burger aficionados. The GBK menu offers classic burger combinations as well as those with more inventive international flavours and diners have the option to create their own. www.gbk.co.uk

TRINITY – ADAM BYATT

Trinity offers the finest in seasonal dining to its decidedly local and loyal clientele in Clapham. Opened in 2006 by Adam Byatt, the neighbourhood gem features a regularly changing à la carte and tasting menu; diners can enjoy both informal yet sophisticated lunches and dinners in the elegantly designed restaurant, which has an open frontage in summer. www.trinityrestaurant.co.uk

VINOTECA– JOHN MURRAY

Top wine bar Vinoteca is renowned for its convivial atmosphere, high-quality wines (more than 25 by the glass and 280 by the bottle) and simple yet imaginative food, created from fresh seasonal produce. Chef John Murray's daily menu delivers this every day, offering dishes inspired by the produce and culinary traditions of Europe's wine-producing regions. www.vinoteca.co.uk

Supporters of The Big Feastival

RACHEL ALLEN

Rachel Allen trained at the Ballymaloe Cookery School, in Ireland, where she still teaches. Her philosophy on food is that good ingredients, simply prepared, will give great results. Her food reflects the demands of her own lifestyle – as a busy working mother, entertaining at home, she produces simple classics with her own unique spin. www.rachelallen.co.uk

SOPHIE GRIGSON

Sophie Grigson is one of Britain's best-loved food writers and television cooks. She is not a chef, but a keen champion of home cooking. She is also patron of the Children's Food Festival. Her new book, *Spices*, will be published in autumn 2011 by Quadrille. Previous books include *The Student Cookbook*, *Eat Your Greens*, and *Sunshine Food*. www.quadrille.co.uk

JO PRATT

Jo Pratt is a food stylist, writer, presenter and home economist. She is the food editor for *Glamour* and is currently working on her fourth book. Jo believes in "real cooking for real people" and has a unique, creative way of home cooking, adapting what she's learnt working alongside Michelin-starred chefs to create everyday recipes that everyone can enjoy at home. www.jopratt.co.uk

THEO RANDALL

Formerly head chef and partner at the River Café, Theo Randall opened his first restaurant, Theo Randall at The InterContinental, in 2008 to overwhelming critical acclaim and success, and he hasn't looked back since. Theo's fast-rising profile in the culinary world has been bolstered by many television appearances and the release of his first book, *Pasta*. www.theorandall.com

THE SHOREDITCH SISTERS

The Shoreditch Sisters were inspired by the creative hub of East London and the ethos of the nationwide Women's Institute to create a space for a community of like-minded women to come together and share their interests and skills. The group was established in 2007 and has grown steadily over the years through word-of-mouth and the help of social media. www.thewi.org.uk

THE WOMEN'S INSTITUTE

The WI has been associated with jam since the organisation's formation in 1915 when members helped preserve precious fruit during the First, and then Second, World Wars. Since then, the WI has been considered an expert in the field of jam-making. Courses for anyone wanting to perfect their jam-making skills are run at the WI's Denman College. www.thewi.org.uk

Big Feastival
big thanks

First of all, we must give a massive shout-out to all of the best talent in Britain for taking the time to support this book. Big thanks to each and every chef and restaurant, as well as all the additional supporters who have provided us with these incredibly delicious recipes. All of the recipes have been donated completely free of charge to help raise those all-important funds for the Jamie Oliver Foundation and The Prince's Trust.

A huge thanks to everyone who was involved in putting this book together. To the amazing Chris Terry for his brilliant food photography, and to his handy sidekicks Steve and Danny: thank you. Thanks to the lovely Sarah Waldie and Philippa Rees and all the guys at Rouge Events for their hard work pulling the content together. And, of course, to Simon Collins and everyone at Superfantastic – James Verity, Mark Arn, Gillian Campbell, Rachael Ball Risk and Steve Pocklington – for the wonderful design of the book.

In-house, thanks to everyone on The Big Feastival team who's helped on the book. To the wonderfully creative Georgie Socratous, gorgeous Jodene Jordan and Jai Harrower for their hard work on the shoot. To the lovely girls Phillippa Spence, Becky Bax and Kate McCullough for their help with recipe testing, and to the fantastic Laura Parr and Mary Lynch for keeping an eye on nutrition. Big shout-out to the lovely girls on words, Rebecca Walker and Tracey Laity, and thanks to the rest of the brilliant team in the office, Claire Postans and Joanne Lord, and the Foundation ladies Liz McMullan and Kate Northrop.

But, most of all, a really big and heartfelt thanks goes to you for buying this lovely cookbook and, in doing so, supporting two fantastic charities. Enjoy The Big Feastival and have a great time in the kitchen recreating these delicious recipes.